T0390264

Invertebrates in the AIR

by
Rebecca Phillips-Bartlett

Minneapolis, Minnesota

Credits
All images are courtesy of Shutterstock.com, unless otherwise specified. With thanks to Getty Images, Thinkstock Photo, and iStockphoto. Recurring images – Aine, Davdeka, top dog, hola.lena, Panuwach, world of vector, Davdeka. Cover – Danut Vieru, unpict, Amalia Gruber, alslutsky, somyot pattana, Aine. 2–3 – Sumruay Rattanataipob. 4–5 – Mikolaj Niemczewski, Nas photo. 6–7 – MeggedyannePhotography, Minko Peev. 8–9 – Achkin, InsectWorld, judyjump. 10–11 – Vineg, Yevhenii Lukashuk. 12–13 – Mr.Samarn Plubkilang, szumimydlo. 14–15 – Georgi Baird, LedyX, FlorencioLeticia. 16–17 – Andi111, Dragomir Radovanovic, world of vector. 18–19 – Ernie Cooper, Waridefia. 20–21 – Davide Bonora, Mariusz Lopusiewicz. 22–23 – Oleg Mikhaylov, Oleksandrum.

Bearport Publishing Company Product Development Team
Publisher: Jen Jenson; Director of Product Development: Spencer Brinker; Managing Editor: Allison Juda; Editor: Cole Nelson; Associate Editor: Naomi Reich; Associate Editor: Tiana Tran; Designer: Kim Jones; Designer: Kayla Eggert; Designer: Steve Scheluchin; Production Specialist: Owen Hamlin

Library of Congress Cataloging-in-Publication Data is available at www.loc.gov or upon request from the publisher.

ISBN: 979-8-89577-018-4 (hardcover)
ISBN: 979-8-89577-449-6 (paperback)
ISBN: 979-8-89577-135-8 (ebook)

© 2026 BookLife Publishing
This edition is published by arrangement with BookLife Publishing.

North American adaptations © 2026 Bearport Publishing Company. All rights reserved. No part of this publication may be reproduced in whole or in part, stored in any retrieval system, or transmitted in any form or by any means, electronic, mechanical, photocopying, recording, or otherwise, without written permission from the publisher. Bearport Publishing is a division of FlutterBee Education Group.

For more information, write to Bearport Publishing, 5357 Penn Avenue South, Minneapolis, MN 55419.

CONTENTS

Minibeasts in the Air 4
Honeybees 6
Mosquitoes 8
Dragonflies 10
Flies .12
Butterflies 14
Flying Ants 16
Grasshoppers 18
Hornets 20
So Many Minibeasts 22
Glossary 24
Index 24

MINIBEASTS
IN THE AIR

Hi! My name is Sammy Swallow. As a bird, I spend most of my time flying through the air. Lots of **invertebrates**, such as **insects**, also fly!

An invertebrate is an animal that has no backbone.

HONEYBEES

Listen closely! Can you hear that buzzing? That's a honeybee. The buzzing comes from the sound of its wings flapping.

Honeybees bring **pollen** from one flower to another. This helps more plants grow.

Honeybees have a special way to **communicate** with one another. They shake their bodies in a special movement called a waggle dance.

Honeybees flap their wings about 200 times a second.

This honeybee is doing a waggle dance.

FACT FILE

Size: Up to 0.75 inches (1.9 cm) long

Diet: Nectar, pollen, and honey

Habitat: Forests, fields, wetlands, and deserts

MOSQUITOES

Many people do not like mosquitoes. Their bites make people itch! Luckily, only some mosquitoes bite to drink blood. Others eat nectar and fruit from plants.

The word *mosquito* means little fly in some languages.

Mosquitoes eat with long, tubelike mouthparts. The insects use them to suck up **liquid** like a straw.

Mouthpart

FACT FILE

Size: Up to 0.75 in. (1.9 cm) long

Diet: Blood, nectar, and fruit

Habitat: Forests, marshes, and grasslands

DRAGONFLIES

Dragonflies can fly forward, backward, straight up, and straight down.

Dragonflies are excellent fliers! They have four wings, and each one can move on its own. This lets dragonflies fly in many different directions.

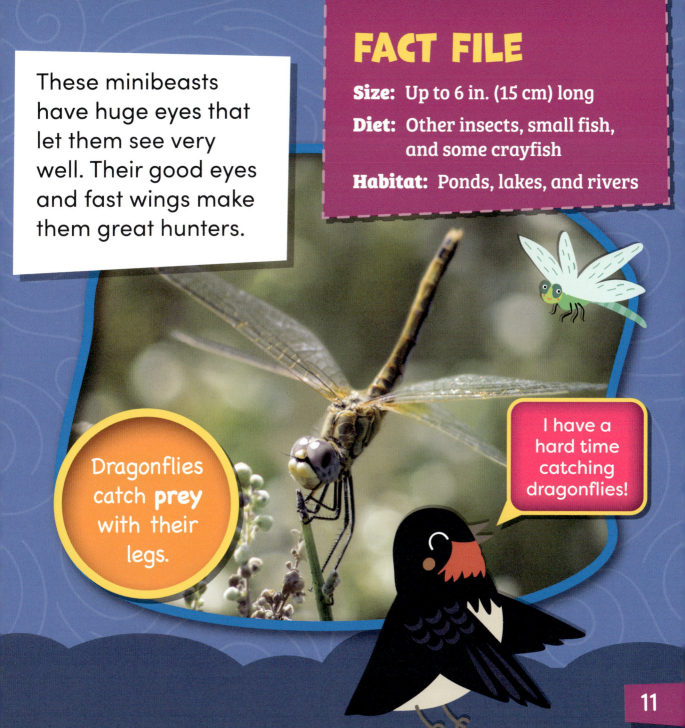

These minibeasts have huge eyes that let them see very well. Their good eyes and fast wings make them great hunters.

FACT FILE

Size: Up to 6 in. (15 cm) long

Diet: Other insects, small fish, and some crayfish

Habitat: Ponds, lakes, and rivers

Dragonflies catch **prey** with their legs.

I have a hard time catching dragonflies!

FLIES

Many minibeasts are called flies. But only some are true flies. True flies have clubs behind each wing.

A fly's clubs help it stay balanced as it flies.

There are so many flavors of flies. *Yum!*

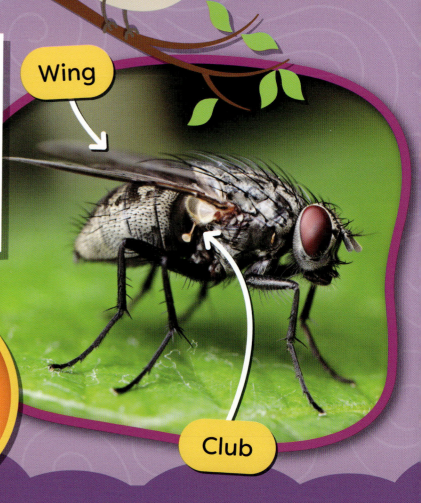

Wing

Club

12

Flies have tiny hairs on the ends of their legs. They use these hairs to find a meal.

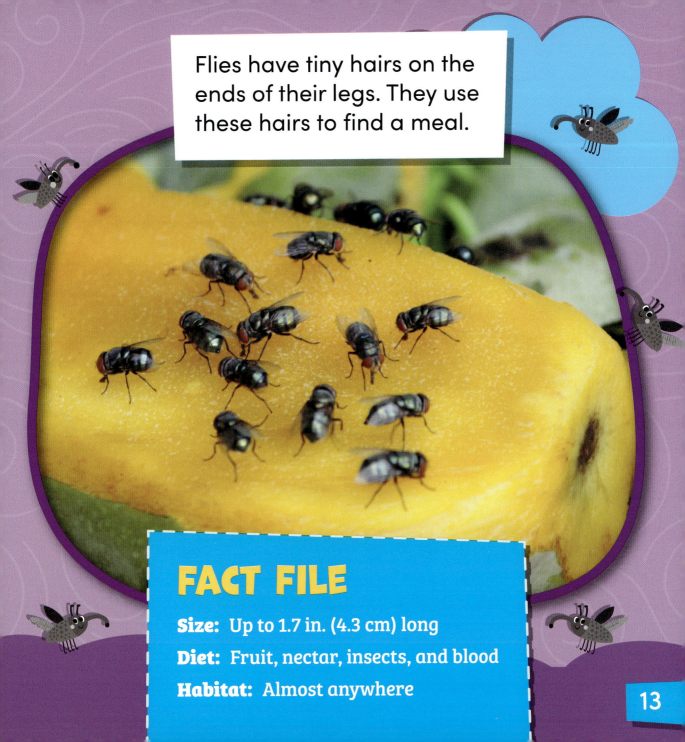

FACT FILE

Size: Up to 1.7 in. (4.3 cm) long

Diet: Fruit, nectar, insects, and blood

Habitat: Almost anywhere

BUTTERFLIES

Many butterflies are brightly colored to stand out. Others use colors to blend in. This is called **camouflage**.

This butterfly's brown wings help it hide.

Butterflies live in many places. However, they prefer warm weather. Some butterflies spend cold months resting.

If it gets too cold, butterflies cannot flap their wings.

FACT FILE

Size: Up to 10.5 in. (26.7 cm) across

Diet: Fruit and nectar

Habitat: Forests, fields, and wetlands

FLYING ANTS

Ants live mostly on the ground. But the drones and queen ants in each **colony** have wings. They are sometimes called flying ants. Queens are the leaders of their colonies.

A queen ant

Each colony has at least one queen. When a new queen is born, she often flies off to start her own colony. Some of the other ants fly with her to look after their new queen.

FACT FILE

Size: Up to 0.6 in. (1.5 cm) long
Diet: Seeds and nectar
Habitat: Most places except polar regions

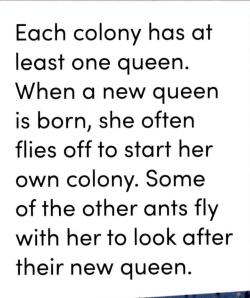

Ants are yummy but tiny!

Drone ants often fly in groups to stay safe.

GRASSHOPPERS

Grasshoppers have wings and very strong back legs. They can fly or jump far away when they see a **predator**.

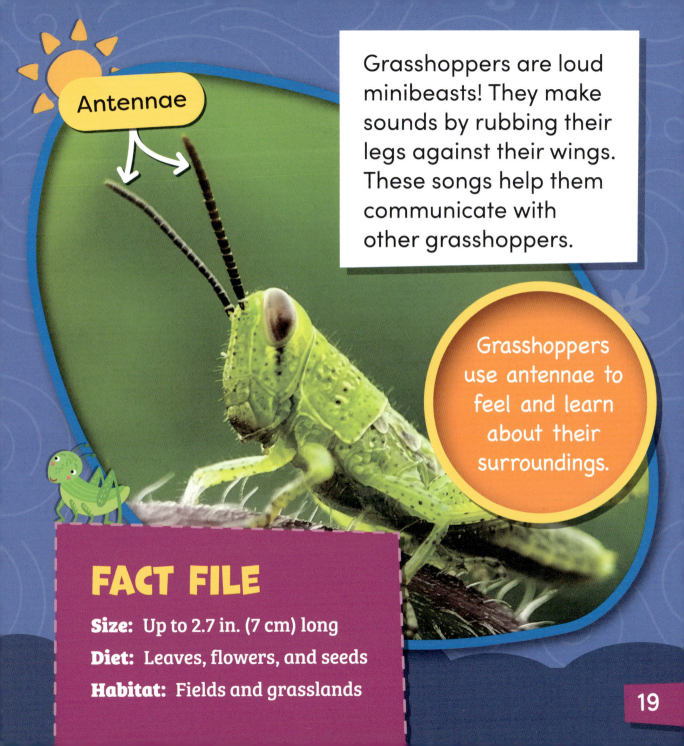

Antennae

Grasshoppers are loud minibeasts! They make sounds by rubbing their legs against their wings. These songs help them communicate with other grasshoppers.

Grasshoppers use antennae to feel and learn about their surroundings.

FACT FILE

Size: Up to 2.7 in. (7 cm) long
Diet: Leaves, flowers, and seeds
Habitat: Fields and grasslands

HORNETS

Hornets are a large type of wasp. They live in groups and create homes called nests.

Hornets have black or brown stripes on their yellow bodies.

20

Hornet nests are made out of chewed-up wood. The insects chew the wood until it becomes soft enough to build with.

FACT FILE

Size: Up to 2 in. (5 cm) long
Diet: Insects, nectar, and fruit
Habitat: Woodlands and fields

Hornets work as a team to build their nests.

Hornet nest

SO MANY MINIBEASTS

So many minibeasts fly through the air. Lots of them fly around doing important jobs. Some bring pollen to plants. Others set up new colonies.

Flying minibeasts are eaten by many animals, including birds, bats, and spiders.

From high up in the sky to just above the ground, the air is full of flying minibeasts. Take a look around! What can you see?

What is your favorite minibeast in the air?

GLOSSARY

camouflage coloring that makes animals blend in with their surroundings

colony a group of the same type of animals that live together

communicate to pass information between two or more things

insects small animals that have six legs, an exoskeleton, two antennae, and three main body parts

invertebrates animals without backbones

liquid a material that flows, such as water

pollen tiny grains that plants make to help grow more plants

predator an animal that hunts other animals for food

prey an animal that is hunted and eaten by other animals

INDEX

bites 8
camouflage 14
colonies 16–17, 22
dances 7
flowers 6
groups 16–17
languages 8
nests 21, 23
plants 6–8, 19, 22
wings 6–7, 10, 12, 14–16, 18